TORNADOES

BILL McAULIFFE

SCIENCE OF THE SKIES

Published by Creative Education
P.O. Box 227, Mankato, Minnesota 56002
Creative Education is an imprint of The Creative Company
www.thecreativecompany.us

Design and production by Liddy Walseth
Art direction by Rita Marshall
Printed by Corporate Graphics in the United States of America

Photographs by Alamy (A.T. Willett), Corbis (Chuck Doswell/Visuals Unlimited,
Eric Nguyen, Jim Reed, Jim Reed/Science Faction, Reuters), Getty Images (Philippe
Bourseiller, John Dominis/Time & Life Pictures, Amber Douthit, Charles Doswell III,
Chris Johns/National Geographic, Miami Herald, Alan R Moller, Panoramic Images,
Carsten Peter, Rich Reid, Silver Screen Collection/Hulton Archive, Topical Press
Agency/Hulton Archive, Stan Wayman/Time & Life Pictures, A.T. Willett), iStockphoto
(Greg Cooksey, Karen Harrison, Sean Martin, Daniel Padavona, Roberto A Sanchez,
Bonnie Schupp, Jeff Smith, Clint Spencer, Victor Zastol'skiy)

Library of Congress Cataloging-in-Publication Data
McAuliffe, Bill.
Tornadoes / by Bill McAuliffe.
p. cm. — (Science of the skies)
Summary: An exploration of tornadoes, including how these frightening storms develop,
how their strength is measured, and how some of the most deadly "twisters" have
impacted human history.
Includes bibliographical references and index.
ISBN 978-1-58341-931-1
1. Tornadoes—Juvenile literature. I. Title. II. Series.

QC955.2.M375 2010
551.55'3—dc22   2009024189

CPSIA: 120109 PO1095

First Edition
2 4 6 8 9 7 5 3 1

TORNADOES

BILL McAULIFFE

SCIENCE OF THE SKIES

WHEN THE TORNADO SIRENS SOUNDED IN GREENSBURG, KANSAS, ON MAY 4, 2007, RESIDENTS WERE READY. AFTER ALL, IT WAS TORNADO SEASON IN TORNADO COUNTRY. MANY OF THEM SCRAMBLED INTO BASEMENTS SPECIALLY REINFORCED TO OFFER PROTECTION FROM TORNADO DAMAGE. BUT WHAT HIT GREENSBURG THAT DAY WAS BEYOND THEIR WORST FEARS. A TORNADO MORE THAN A MILE AND A HALF (2.4 KM) WIDE—WIDER THAN GREENSBURG ITSELF—POUNCED ON THE LITTLE CITY. SPINNING WITH WINDS IN EXCESS OF 200 MILES (320 KM) PER HOUR, THE FUNNEL LEFT LITTLE MORE THAN THE GRAIN ELEVATOR STANDING IN THE TOWN OF 1,500 RESIDENTS. TEN PEOPLE WERE KILLED. "IT WAS LIKE THE BOMBING OF HIROSHIMA," SAID ONE RESIDENT, REFERRING TO THE DROPPING OF A NUCLEAR BOMB IN WORLD WAR II. FEW TORNADOES ARE AS STRONG AS THE GREENSBURG MONSTER. AND ALTHOUGH RESEARCHERS CONTINUE TO LEARN MORE ABOUT THEM, TWISTERS REMAIN ONE OF NATURE'S MOST FEARED AND MYSTERIOUS FORCES.

THE TWISTING TERROR

Tornadoes have terrified humans through the ages. Dropping from the sky in dark, thick columns or ratlike tails, the funnels often make a nightmarish impression with shrieking sounds and enough power to lift buildings off their foundations, toss railroad cars, or drive pieces of straw through tree trunks. They can destroy one home and kill everyone inside without breaking a window on the house next door.

Despite their destructive potential, tornadoes still aren't fully understood. Difficult to predict, hard to find, and dangerous to be near, twisters are very challenging to study. Until recently, most scientific instruments lucky enough to get in the way of one simply got blown away. Indeed, tornadoes remain "one of the last frontiers of **atmospheric** science," writes **meteorologist** and author Howard Bluestein.

Eyewitness accounts of tornadoes as far back as 1759 in New England make note of how clouds blowing from different directions converged to form something called a "land hurricane." Later, in the 1800s, some scientists believed tornadoes were generated by electrical forces from the railroads and telegraph wires that crossed the landscape. For a time, tornadoes came to be regarded as simply too scarce to be studied. And from 1887 to 1950, the word "tornado" was banned from forecasts by United States government agencies.

Officials thought the predictions would terrify citizens rather than help them.

World War II gave birth to new technology and a heightened interest in forecasting, which helped meteorologists understand more about tornadoes. The first accurate prediction of a tornado was issued (though not publicly) in 1948 at Oklahoma's Tinker Air Force Base—though it is now regarded as having been a matter of coincidence, if not nearly impossible good luck. Five years later, meteorologists in Illinois first detected one of the telltale electronic signs of a tornado—a hook shape within a storm—on **radar**. But **hook echoes** sometimes appeared when a tornado didn't, or didn't appear when a tornado did. Forecasters still needed someone outdoors to lay eyes on a tornado before they issued a warning.

Tornadoes may be the world's most terrifying storms; as they snake down out of the sky and then whirl across miles of land, they can seem like monsters.

The radar of the 1950s, which produced images that were merely green blobs, detected only rain or hail. In 1958, meteorologists began to use **Doppler radar**, which police had been using since 1954 to detect speeding drivers. That may have been the single greatest advance in tornado detection. Doppler radar measures how fast rain in an approaching storm is moving toward the radar antenna. Even more importantly, it can also measure the speed of rain moving away from the antenna in the same approaching storm. If those two motions occur within the same storm, it means the storm is rotating and very possibly could produce a tornado. Doppler radar has allowed forecasters sometimes to sound a tornado warning before anyone on the ground has even seen one.

What is known for certain is that the creation of a tornado nearly always requires a thunderstorm. The U.S. National Severe Storms Laboratory, which is based in Norman, Oklahoma, in the heart of **Tornado Alley**, estimates that 2,000 thunderstorms are battering Earth at any given moment. But it's the rare **supercell** thunderstorm—2 out of those 2,000—that is most likely to produce a damaging tornado. One of every five or six supercells throws down a tornado.

Like all thunderstorms, supercells are marked by an updraft of warm air that cools as it rises and **condenses**

Doppler weather radar, which utilizes antenna towers like this one, is today one of the most important technologies involved in tornado detection and research.

TORNADO WANNABES

Several natural phenomena are similar to tornadoes, though not as destructive. Waterspouts are tornadoes over water—perhaps 50 yards (45 m) wide at most—that dissipate over land. Dust devils develop in desert areas when the ground heats up, causing dust to swirl upward. Being in the desert, they're not attached to clouds, and their wind speeds are slower than those in weak tornadoes. Forest fires can often produce a whirl of smoke and fire with winds of 100 miles (160 km) per hour. "Gustnadoes," meanwhile, are swirls of dust that rise in the gust front of a thunderstorm, but they are not tornadoes.

One of the most remarkable traits of tornadoes is the way in which they can stretch horizontally; such tornadoes are usually weaker than purely vertical ones.

into rain, hail, snow, or ice. But in a supercell, the updrafts can move at tremendous speeds—150 miles (241 km) per hour or more. At the same time, winds surrounding the storm at ground level and at various heights often move in different directions from one another or at different speeds. The latest theories on how tornadoes form point to this type of **wind shear** as one of the keys.

Remarkably, it's now believed that tornadoes might also develop from something like large-**diameter** tubes of air rolling horizontally along the ground. If air blows fast enough over the air level below it, it can curl into such a tube, like a breaking wave. Cold air jutting underneath warm air can also get a tube rolling. If this tube encounters the thunderstorm's updraft, it can be tipped upward, ultimately causing a broad, rotating **mesocyclone** within the supercell. This whirling mass of clouds often gets most organized between 15,000 and 20,000 feet (4,600–6,100 m) and is often several miles wide.

It's believed that about 30 percent of mesocyclones produce tornadoes, but there are different theories about just how it happens. Warm air twisting upward into the mesocyclone will cool as it rises, condensing into rain. Some scientists believe that as the supply of ground-level warm air dwindles, the updraft sucks

This 2003 mesocyclone over South Dakota spawned more than a dozen tornadoes; although no twisters are pictured here, the cloud rotation is clearly visible.

air upward even more forcefully in an attempt to feed itself. This tightens and speeds up the rotation, much like a figure skater pulling in his or her arms, and eventually forms a funnel that reaches down to the ground—a tornado.

But other forces are thought to work in different ways to produce a twister. In the broad mesocyclone, the sinking of rain-cooled air can drag the entire circulation toward the ground. In other circumstances, low **air pressure** at ground level—nearly a vacuum—can pull a spinning funnel from the clouds to the ground.

Sometimes the airborne forces can spin with such power that they suck dust and debris off the ground into the air, without any apparent connection to the dark clouds above. In other cases, a **vortex** of rain will drop toward the ground as it feeds on warm, humid air below. This condensation funnel is visible from its wide top to its narrow tip because it consists of rain, which makes it appear dark in color. But no funnel is officially a tornado until it connects the sky with the ground.

There is much about these complicated, ferocious forces of nature that remains unknown. With computers, radar-equipped vehicles, more organized teams of storm spotters and chasers, and demands for increasingly accurate predictions, researchers are learning more about tornadoes with every storm season.

Tornadoes can be strikingly different in form, from snaking funnels (below) that seem to loosely link earth and sky, to broad twisters that drop heavily from supercells (right).

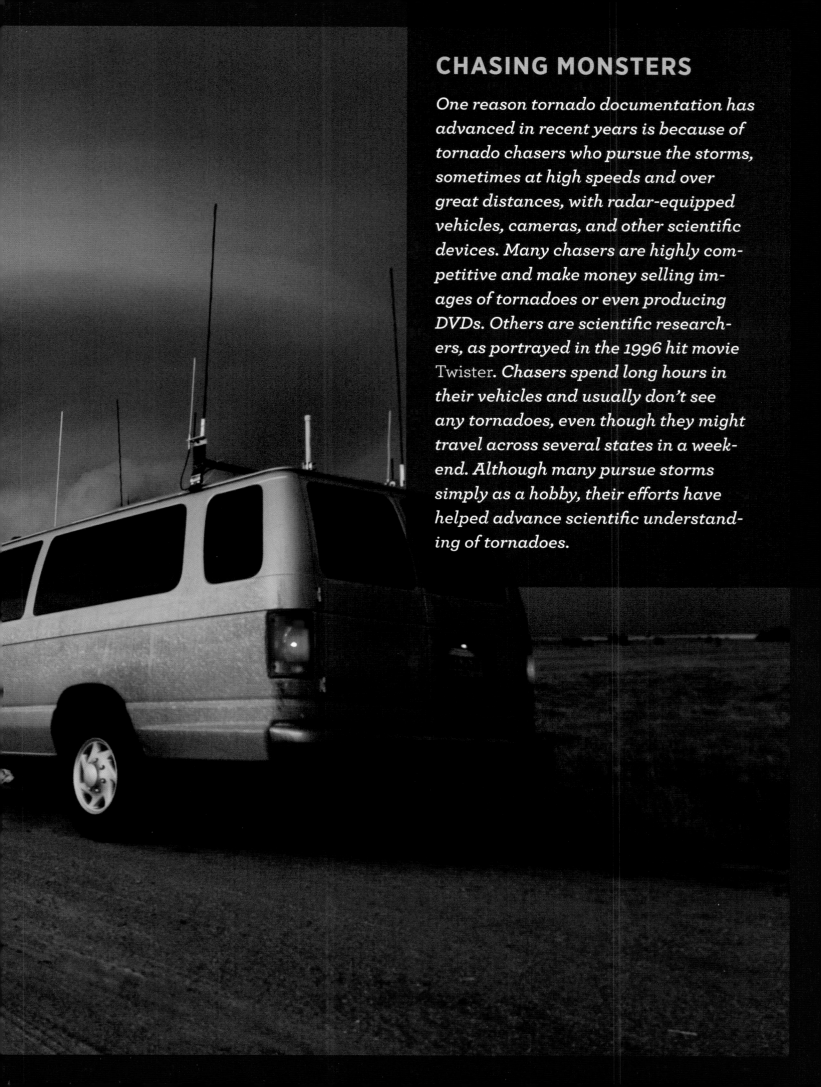

CHASING MONSTERS

One reason tornado documentation has advanced in recent years is because of tornado chasers who pursue the storms, sometimes at high speeds and over great distances, with radar-equipped vehicles, cameras, and other scientific devices. Many chasers are highly competitive and make money selling images of tornadoes or even producing DVDs. Others are scientific researchers, as portrayed in the 1996 hit movie Twister. Chasers spend long hours in their vehicles and usually don't see any tornadoes, even though they might travel across several states in a weekend. Although many pursue storms simply as a hobby, their efforts have helped advance scientific understanding of tornadoes.

SPINNING INTO HISTORY

The deadliest tornado in recorded history is believed to be one that devastated part of Bangladesh on April 26, 1989. Tearing a swath 1 mile (1.6 km) wide, it killed an estimated 1,300 people in the densely populated Asian nation, injured 12,000, and left 80,000 homeless as it destroyed 2 entire cities.

In the U.S., a tornado that dropped out of the clouds over Missouri on March 18, 1925, ranks as the deadliest ever to hit the nation. Everything about it was remarkable—the strength of its winds, its width, the distance it traveled on the ground, and its speed. Known as the Tri-State Tornado, this terrible twister carved out a chilling story as it spun its way into history.

The Tri-State Tornado first touched down near Ellington, Missouri, in the state's rural southeastern corner, at 1:01 P.M. Moving east-northeast, it destroyed about 90 percent of Annapolis, Missouri, 15 minutes later. Just before 2:30 P.M., having killed 13 people already in Missouri, it crossed the Mississippi River into Illinois as an engine of death and destruction.

Sometimes traveling faster than 70 miles (113 km) per hour, nearly twice as fast as tornadoes usually move, the three-quarter-mile-wide (1.2 km) tornado sprang on its victims before they could react. It was that reason, along with the lightly built housing of the time and the lack of any organized warning system, that explained the high death toll. With spinning winds estimated at 300 miles (483 km) per hour, the tornado appeared more like a dark wall than a funnel, according to accounts. There are no pictures of the giant tornado. Amid such sudden upheaval, it's unlikely anyone who even had a camera in those days had time to reach for it.

The middle of the U.S.—known in a weather context as Tornado Alley—is the most tornado-infested place on Earth, spawning such twisters as this one on the Texas prairie.

In the next 40 minutes, this whirling monster killed 541 people, including 37 at Gorham, Illinois, which was completely leveled. At Murphysboro, 234 died, the most in any single city in a U.S. tornado, even though it was a relatively small farming community. At neighboring DeSoto, 33 were killed in a single school, also the worst natural disaster of its kind in the U.S. At West Frankfort, Illinois, 148 were killed, but that number could have been much higher had 800 miners not been far below ground at the time. Their good fortune was limited, though; many emerged from the mine to find loved ones killed and homes obliterated.

At about 4:00 P.M., the tornado crossed the Wabash River into Indiana, destroying the town of Griffin. By the time the tornado vanished at 4:30 P.M., about 695 people in 3 states lay dead or about to die from injuries. The tornado's 3 hours and 29 minutes on the ground, as well as its 217-mile-long (349 km) path, have never been exceeded by any U.S. twister.

Children are here shown sitting amid the wreckage left by 1925's Tri-State Tornado in Murphysboro, Illinois; 32 years later, the town was hit by another twister.

A BULL'S-EYE IN TORNADO ALLEY

Codell, Kansas, and its surroundings were hit by tornadoes on the same date three years in a row: May 20 of 1916, 1917, and 1918. The 1916 tornado, an F2, struck three miles (4.8 km) east of town with little damage. The 1917 twister was an immense F3 that ran two miles (3.2 km) west of town, destroying six farmsteads. But these were just warm-ups. The 1918 tornado was an F4 that tore right through town, leveling two churches, a school, and much of the downtown. It killed 9 people in a 60-mile (96 km) path. Residents of Codell later marked every May 20 as Cyclone Day.

This tornado offered evidence against a common myth by spinning through downtown Miami, Florida, in May 1997, injuring five people and causing minor damage.

One popular myth about tornadoes is that they don't strike cities. It might better be said that tornadoes don't strike cities *often*, and that's true for two simple reasons: tornadoes are small, as storms go, and there simply aren't many large cities on the Great Plains, the area of the central U.S. where twisters are most common.

Still, it's curious that this idea ever became popular, since the city of St. Louis, Missouri, has been slammed by tornadoes 10 times since 1871. A tornado on May 27, 1896, killed 255 people in St. Louis and neighboring East St. Louis, Illinois, making it the third-deadliest tornado on record in America. (Second, after the Tri-State Tornado, was the Natchez, Mississippi, tornado of May 7, 1840, which killed 317 people.) The twister may have also been the costliest. Converted to modern dollar values, the damage it caused has been estimated to have reached nearly $3 billion.

St. Louis was one of the nation's most populated cities at the time and was crowded with visitors and citizens preparing for the Republican National Convention when the tornado touched down about six miles (9.6 km) west of downtown. Soon it was about a mile (1.6 km) wide. When it reached the Eads Bridge over the Mississippi River, it was at its strongest. According to tornado expert Thomas Grazulis,

Farmers and ranchers on the Great Plains—especially in the states of Texas, Oklahoma, and Kansas—can do little against tornadoes except hope the storms miss them.

it was there that a 2-inch by 10-inch (5 by 25 cm) pine plank was driven through an iron plate 5/16-inch (.8 cm) thick. (The bridge wasn't severely damaged; fortunately, it had been reinforced after being hit by a tornado 26 years earlier.) The tornado killed 137 people in St. Louis, then obliterated buildings and homes along the Mississippi River before killing another 118 people in East St. Louis. Some believe that, similar to the Natchez tornado, many more victims weren't counted because they were probably swept down the river. Many people thought the political convention should be moved to a different city, but it was held as scheduled only three weeks later, despite the damage to the city.

April 3, 1974, was the deadliest day for tornadoes in U.S. history. A terrifying total of 147 tornadoes touched down in 13 states in 16 hours (and 1 more just across the Michigan–Canadian border), killing 330 people. All of the tornadoes were east of the Mississippi River, and the concentration extended due north: from northern Alabama and Georgia through Tennessee, and from Kentucky through Indiana. Six twisters were rated F5— the most destructive. On average, only one F5 tornado is spawned in the U.S. in an entire year. The tornadoes tore across a combined total of 2,014 miles (3,241 km) of ground. Forty-eight of the tornadoes were killers.

Alabama suffered 86 deaths, the most of any state that day, while 34 died in the city of Xenia, Ohio.

The 1974 outbreak led the National Weather Service to improve its radar systems and computerized storm modeling. It also marked the beginning of the ratings system for tornado strength that is still in use today. Joseph Shaefer, director of the National Oceanographic and Atmospheric Association (NOAA) Storm Prediction Center in Norman, Oklahoma, described it years later as a freakishly rare event. "There's never been anything like it before, as far as we know, or since," he said.

Tornado-induced misery in places such as St. Louis, Missouri (pictured, top, after a 1959 twister), helped encourage the development of radar technology (bottom).

05/08/86
18:22:25

0   <TH
1   RF
2   -32
3   -28
4   -23
5   -18
6   -13
7   - 7
8   0
9   + 7
A   +13
B   +18
C   +23
D   +28
E   +32
F   R10
CAZ=055
CRG=035
SM=15e220
AZ+=048
RG+=033
HT+=02.3

UNSAFETY TIPS

Some of the most commonly heard tornado safety tips are old wives' tales. Opening windows to balance indoor and outdoor air pressure is useless when a tornado approaches. People should get away from windows, which will probably break anyway. Also, highway overpasses are not good places to hide; winds will often actually increase in speed to get under a bridge. And unless you're traveling away from the funnel, a car is not a safe place to be. Cars can be tossed and crushed in a tornado. Of the 42 people killed in a 1979 tornado in Wichita Falls, Texas, more than half were in cars.

LIVING
DANGEROUSLY

The number of tornadoes has been increasing in recent decades, particularly in the U.S. and Canada, but probably only because there are more people in more places to see them. Also, storm chasers and news reporters, equipped with tornado-tracking radar, are increasingly eager to see and photograph or videotape tornadoes. So naturally, more and more tornadoes are being documented and even posted as videos on Internet sites such as YouTube. But meteorologists believe that many more tornadoes are never even counted. Those are the ones that skim across remote areas, or hide by night or in the darkness of storms and do little damage.

The U.S. gets strafed by about 1,000 tornadoes a year. That seems like a huge number, and it is greater than the number that hits any other nation on the planet. But tornadoes are actually quite rare in the sense that few people ever witness one.

Tornadoes have occurred in every state in the U.S. and visit the Canadian prairie provinces of Alberta, Manitoba, and Saskatchewan nearly every year. The Netherlands, a small but densely populated country, has the highest occurrence of tornadoes per person of any nation in the world. Tornadoes also touch down in Great Britain, Bangladesh, northern Argentina, southern Brazil, southern Russia, and Australia. Those are

generally flat places, but tornadoes have also been documented at high altitudes in California mountains.

Still, the central plains of the U.S. is the only place in the world known as Tornado Alley, and for good reason. The vast, open expanse is a battleground for continent-sized air masses. Often, warm, moist air from the Gulf of Mexico and cooler, dry air from the Rocky Mountains will clash there, creating chains of thunderstorms hundreds of miles long. And thunderstorms, of course, are where tornadoes are born.

Even though North American tornadoes favor the plains, the continent's mountainous regions are not immune, as this 2008 twister in Colorado demonstrated.

But there's an additional feature that makes the Great Plains prone to tornadoes. Cool and dry air coming off the high-altitude deserts and mountains to the west often streams at a higher altitude than the warm, moist air moving northward from the Gulf of Mexico. While the warm air wants to rise—warm air *always* wants to rise—it can be capped by the cooler air above. But not forever. Like steam in a pressure cooker, the rising warm air can build up such force that it bursts through the cap of cool air. It's this rapid rising that can lead to large hailstones, heavy rain, and the violent air movement that can produce tornadoes.

It's fortunate that the Great Plains region is not as heavily populated as the U.S. coasts or Great Lakes area, because when tornadoes strike populated areas, they can cause tremendous damage and misery. Still, the growth of U.S. cities and towns has presented ever-bigger targets to tornadoes.

Most people who live in tornado-prone areas know they're supposed to head for the basement or an interior room when they hear a tornado warning. But that's a key reason why tornadoes kill so many people in mobile homes; these types of homes have neither

basements nor interior rooms. Some mobile home communities have group shelters, but these may not be close enough for residents to reach quickly. Mobile homes are sometimes required to have **tie-downs** to keep the structure from tumbling away. But the straps and anchors frequently fail, and the homes themselves are not strong enough to withstand tornado-force winds. There are 20 times as many tornado deaths in mobile homes as there are in homes built on permanent foundations, according to the NOAA's National Severe Storms Laboratory.

Still, because tornadoes are relatively small and **capricious**, buildings even in high-risk areas do not always have strong tornado protection. For example, tornado experts believe that a wide door on an attached garage in front of a home is a place where tornado winds can easily break into a home and explode it from the inside out. Yet this continues to be a popular home design.

Some cities in tornado-prone areas from Oklahoma to Ohio require home builders to install special connectors between the sides of a house and its foundation to help keep the building in place during high winds. Other strengthening features might include rigid connectors between the walls and the roof, to help keep the roof attached. But they're not always required, and

Although storm shelters (above) offer no guarantees of safety under tornado-producing storms, they have long given people at least a measure of protection.

STAYING SAFE IN A TORNADO

Safety experts say that in stormy weather, people should first tune into news media or a NOAA weather radio. They shouldn't wait to hear sirens, since tornadoes can form before a warning can be sounded. Also, people indoors might not even hear a siren. If tornadoes approach, people should head for a basement or an interior room, and get under a table or mattress or into a bathtub. Drivers should travel perpendicular to the path of a tornado, if possible, or leave their vehicles and get into a building. People caught outside should get into a low area, lie flat, and cover their heads.

some builders don't install them because they make the house more expensive to construct. A common argument against such requirements is that few structures can withstand a direct hit from a tornado without major damage, no matter what safety features they might have.

But in some areas—Oklahoma and Texas primarily—many homeowners are today adding safe rooms to their homes. Safe rooms, where residents can go if a tornado is coming, are usually in the interior of a house, away from windows and outside walls, and often have everyday uses as bathrooms or closets. Their walls and ceilings are reinforced to prevent objects or heavy water from collapsing them. They're also bolted down so they can't topple. Researchers at Texas Tech University determined that a safe room offers adequate protection if it can withstand winds of 250 miles (402 km) per hour and can't be penetrated by a 2-inch by 4-inch (5 by 10 cm) piece of lumber fired at it at a speed of 100 miles (160 km) per hour. Following a devastating tornado outbreak in Kansas and Oklahoma in 1999, money from government grants helped thousands of homeowners build safe rooms in their homes. In many cases, safe rooms remain standing after all the houses in a neighborhood are otherwise reduced to rubble.

A tornado's highly concentrated winds can overpower nearly any building except the most solid of safe rooms, turning lumber and other items into potentially lethal projectiles.

Despite irregular safety requirements and the fact that more and more people are living in the paths of tornadoes, the tornado death rates are declining. An average of 112 people were killed by tornadoes in the U.S. annually from 1950 through 1979, but since then, the average has been about 54, or less than half what it was before. In 1925, there were 1.8 tornado deaths per one million people in the U.S.; by 2000, that figure had dropped to 0.12. Most credit Doppler radar, more warning time or better detection, and improved communications for reducing the fatalities.

In the Tri-State Tornado of 1925, a pair of pants reportedly flew 39 miles (63 km) with $95 in the pocket. A wedding dress drifted 50 miles (80 km) in Massachusetts in 1953, being found in "surprisingly good condition," according to one historian. A golf course flag traveled 43 miles (69 km) across Oklahoma in May 1995. The distance record, according to tornado expert Thomas Grazulis in his 2001 book The Tornado, is 223 (359 km) miles, held by a personal check that traveled from Stockton, Kansas, to Winnetoon, Nebraska, on April 11, 1991. For a person, the airborne record is 1 mile (1.6 km), with a fatal crash landing.

CROSS-COUNTRY BY AIR

TAKING
TORNADOES'
MEASURE

Tornadoes are most often measured in three ways: how wide they are, how far they travel, and how fast their spinning winds are moving. A tornado at Blair, Oklahoma, in 1928 might have been an astonishing seven miles (11.2 km) wide, though some **straight-line wind** damage may have been included in that figure. In recent decades, the maximum width appears to be about two miles (3.2 km). The most recent record-holder was the Hallam, Nebraska, tornado of May 22, 2004, which was about 2.5 miles (4 km) wide. The average width of all tornadoes, of course, is much smaller: 300 to 500 yards (275–460 m).

The 217 miles (349 km) that the Tri-State Tornado traveled remains the known record for distance covered by a twister. The U.S. Federal Emergency Management Agency states that for the 2 percent of tornadoes that are the most destructive, the average trip covers 26 miles (42 km).

But when it comes to measuring a tornado's strength, it's all about wind speed. The highest wind speeds ever recorded on Earth occurred in a tornado that killed 36 people in and near Oklahoma City on May 3, 1999. A mobile Doppler radar rig measured winds in the tornado at between 281 and 321 miles (452–517 km) per hour. Ultimately, the tornado caused $1.1 billion in damage, making it also the costliest in U.S.

history. As remarkable as the wind measurement was, it left one question unanswered. Those winds were 105 feet (32 m) above the ground. No one has yet measured winds in a tornado precisely at ground level, where they might be slowed by **friction** against the ground and other structures.

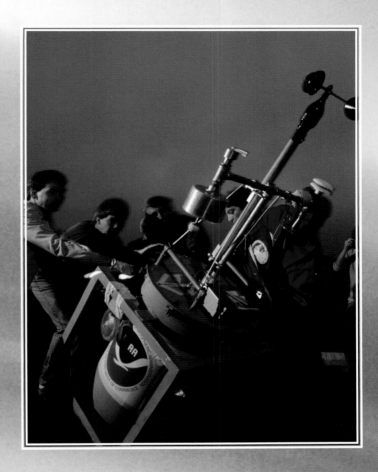

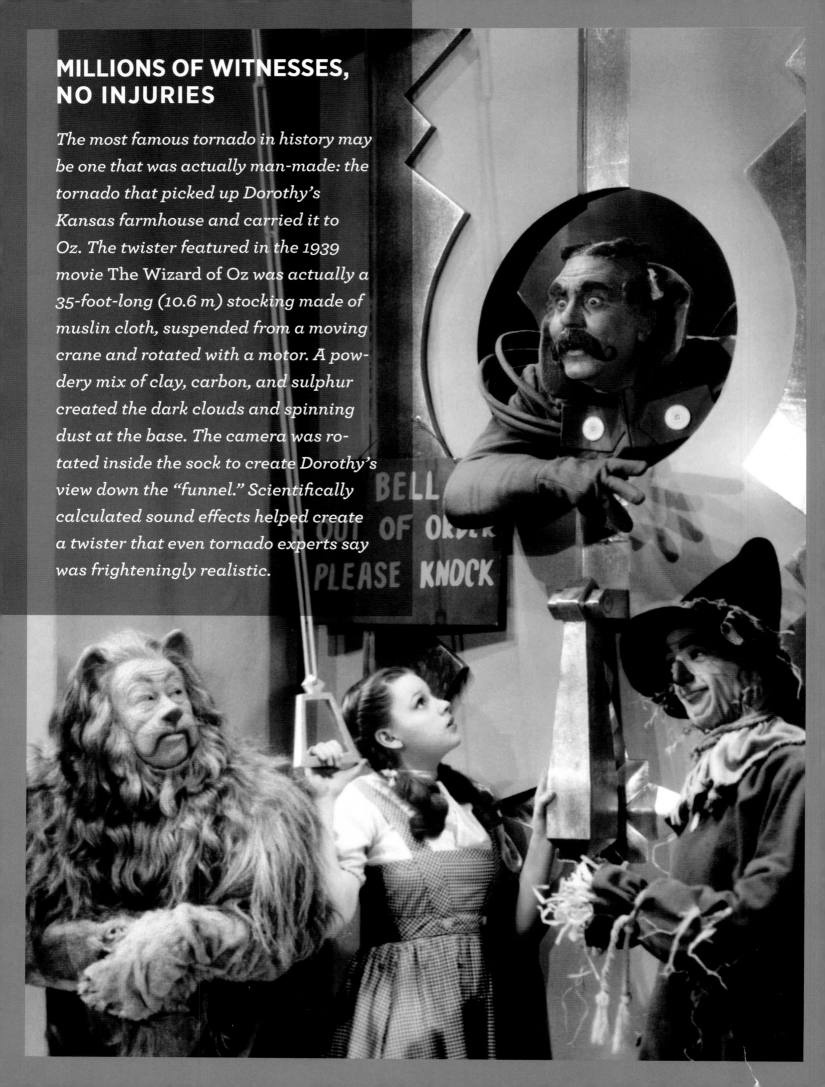

MILLIONS OF WITNESSES, NO INJURIES

The most famous tornado in history may be one that was actually man-made: the tornado that picked up Dorothy's Kansas farmhouse and carried it to Oz. The twister featured in the 1939 movie The Wizard of Oz *was actually a 35-foot-long (10.6 m) stocking made of muslin cloth, suspended from a moving crane and rotated with a motor. A powdery mix of clay, carbon, and sulphur created the dark clouds and spinning dust at the base. The camera was rotated inside the sock to create Dorothy's view down the "funnel." Scientifically calculated sound effects helped create a twister that even tornado experts say was frighteningly realistic.*

Once they analyze the damage at the school, assessors will move on to other types of structures on their checklist: homes, motels, shopping malls, and power line towers, for example. Trees get a look, too. The damage and wind speeds are then lined up with the EF Scale to determine a value for the tornado's strength, though the final rating goes to the highest estimated wind along the twister's path:

ESTIMATED WIND SPEED	EF RATING
65 to 85 miles (105–137 km) per hour	EF0
86 to 110 miles (138–177 km) per hour	EF1
111 to 135 miles (178–217 km) per hour	EF2
136 to 165 miles (218–266 km) per hour	EF3
166 to 200 miles (267–322 km) per hour	EF4
Over 200 miles (322 km) per hour	EF5

One problem with the EF Scale is that there aren't as many objects to be damaged by a tornado in open country as there are in a developed area. That means there are fewer examples to help determine a tornado's strength in a rural area. But experts are continuing to analyze damage to crops, farm equipment, **irrigation** devices, and other agricultural features that might help with such calculations.

Indeed, it was storm damage to a wheat field that led to one of the best looks anyone has ever had of a tornado. Kansas farmer Will Keller was out looking at what hail had done to his crop when he heard a "screaming, hissing sound" and looked up into the

IT SOUNDED LIKE ...

A freight train. An 18-wheeler. A waterfall. A swarm of bees. The sound of a tornado is often what people describe as one of its most extraordinary and frightening features. Scientists believe that each tornado produces its own signature sound, which may be generated by the interaction of high-speed winds with the surface of the land or buildings, by the swirl and clatter of debris, or by the swinging funnel itself. Researchers are also studying how sounds from tornadoes that are below the range of human hearing may be detected by special devices to signal that a tornado is coming.

heart of a funnel 50 to 100 yards (46–91 m) wide. The year was 1928, and Keller didn't need the Fujita Scale or an understanding of wind shear and updrafts to describe the snakelike vision in astonishing terms. Luckily for him, the funnel wasn't in contact with the ground. Seventy-nine years later, people not far from his farm near Greensburg, Kansas, had a much different encounter with a much different tornado and saw more than they wanted to see—their town wiped away.

As long as tornadoes continue to descend from the sky, people will fear these spinning giants—and potentially face the prospect of rebuilding homes and communities.

GLOSSARY

AIR PRESSURE, n. — *the force of a column of air, which has weight, over a particular location*

ATMOSPHERIC, adj. — *having to do with the atmosphere, the layer of gases that surrounds Earth*

CAPRICIOUS, adj. — *unpredictable or erratic*

CONDENSES, v. — *forms a liquid from a vapor*

DIAMETER, n. — *the widest distance across a circle or through a ball*

DOPPLER RADAR, n. — *radar that measures the speed of moving objects, named after Austrian scientist Christian Doppler*

ESTIMATORS, n. — *analysts from the National Weather Service who tour sites of tornado damage to determine how strong the storms were*

FRICTION, n. — *the rubbing or resistance of one object or surface against another*

HOOK ECHOES, n. — *electronic images, created by the bounce-back of a radar beam from a storm, that often indicate the formation of a tornado*

IRRIGATION, n. — *a process that draws water from underground or from streams and rivers and spreads it over farm fields*

MESOCYCLONE, n. — *a rotating area of a thunderstorm, two to six miles (3–10 km) in diameter and about five miles (8 km) above the ground, in which tornadoes often form*

METEOROLOGIST, n. — *a scientist who studies weather patterns, weather phenomena, and other behaviors of the atmosphere*

RADAR, n. — *a system that uses radio waves bounced off objects, such as planes or raindrops, to determine their location, size, and speed; the word stands for Radio Detecting and Ranging*

STRAIGHT-LINE WIND, n. — *damaging wind that moves in one direction, unlike the circular winds of tornadoes*

SUPERCELL, n. — *part of a system of thunderstorms that develops in such a way that it can continue to feed itself on updrafts of warm, moist air*

TIE-DOWNS, n. — *straps or other devices connected to buried anchors to help keep mobile homes in place during high winds*

TORNADO ALLEY, n. — *an area of the central U.S., running roughly from Texas and Oklahoma north to the Dakotas and east to Ohio, that experiences the greatest number of tornadoes in the world*

VORTEX, n. — *in weather terms, a whirling mass of air*

WIND SHEAR, n. — *a clash of winds moving in different directions or at different speeds, often at different levels, which can cause rotation in a storm*

Bluestein, Howard B. *Tornado Alley: Monster Storms of the Great Plains*. New York: Oxford University Press, 1999.

Farndon, John. *Extreme Weather*. London: Dorling Kindersley, 2007.

Galvin, John. "Super Tornado Outbreak: Miss. and Ohio River Valleys, April 1974." *Popular Mechanics*, July 31, 2007. http://www.popularmechanics.com/science/worst_case_scenarios/4219870.html?page=1.

Grazulis, Thomas P. *The Tornado: Nature's Ultimate Windstorm*. Norman, Okla.: University of Oklahoma Press, 2001.

National Oceanic and Atmospheric Administration. *Advanced Spotters' Field Guide*. Washington, D.C.: U.S. Department of Commerce, 2008.

National Severe Storms Laboratory. "Severe Weather Primer: Tornado Basics." National Oceanic and Atmospheric Administration. http://www.nssl.noaa.gov/primer/tornado/tor_basics.html.

National Weather Service Storm Prediction Center. "The Basics about Tornadoes." National Oceanic and Atmospheric Administration. http://www.spc.noaa.gov/faq/tornado/#The%20Basics.

Tornado Project Online. "Homepage." http://www.tornadoproject.com.

INDEX